2020

Joy ~

please know

you are loved by so

many, including me!

Sue ♥

Sue Coccia

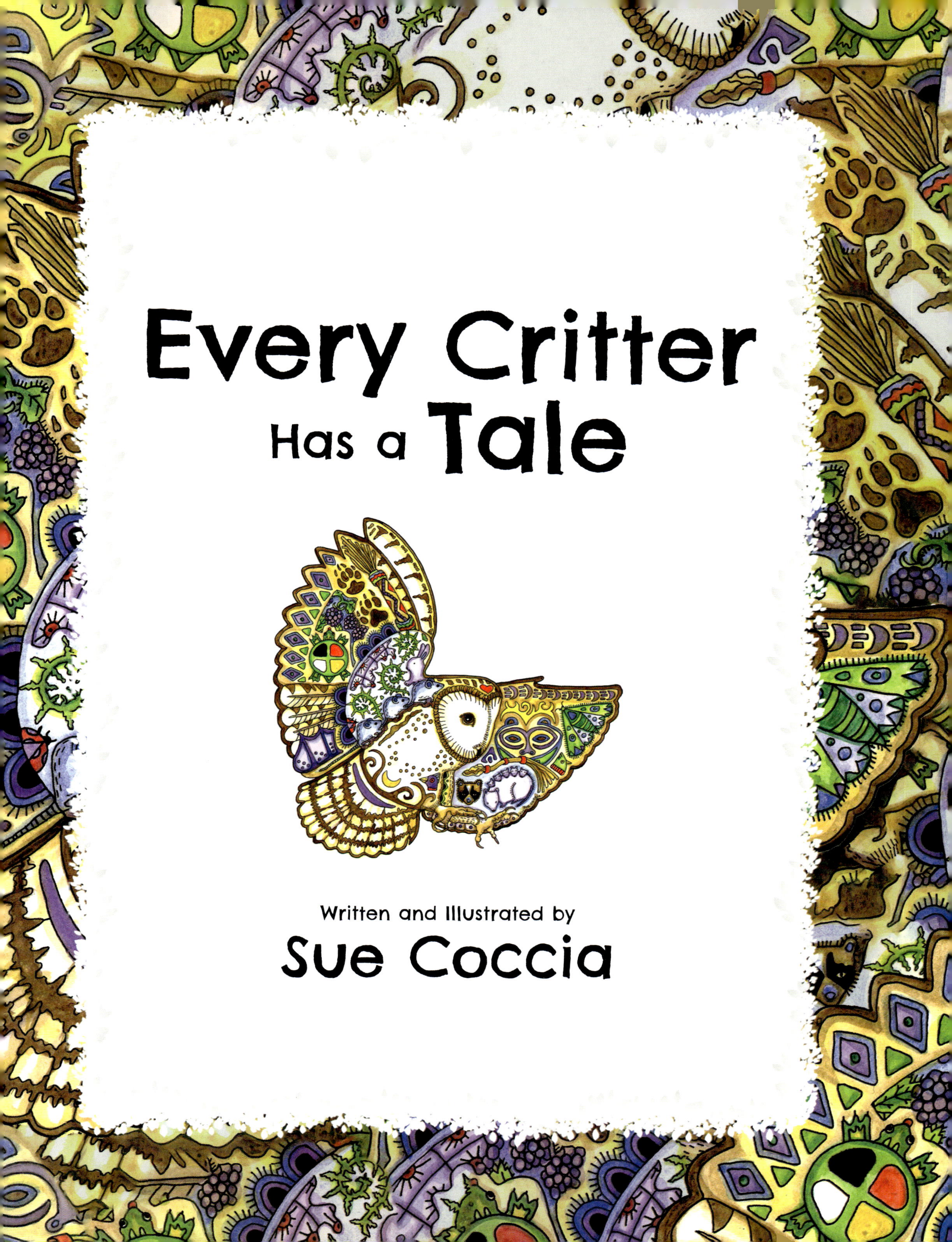

Every Critter Has a Tale

Written and Illustrated by

Sue Coccia

ISBN: 978-1-59849-276-7
Library of Congress Control Number: 2019917760

Printed in the United States of America

Editor: Danielle Harvey
Design: Soundview Design

www.earthartinternational.com

Requests for such permissions should be addressed to:

Peanut Butter Publishing
943 NE Boat Street
Seattle, Washington 98105
206-860-4900
www.peanutbutterpublishing.com

SFI label applies to the text stock

This book is dedicated to the animals and the environments they live in, as we are all connected.

SUE COCCIA

Acknowledgements

I'd like to give thanks to

Silvana Iosue for her graphic design
and coordination

My husband, Frank ~ my muse

My son, Frank

My daughter, Gina, and my son in law, Josh

My fabulous grandkids,
Niko,
Mila,
and Jozi.

And a special thanks to my RHS friend and
author Dan Raley, who helped edit this story
and encouraged us to see it through.

You may think this story is only about Bear. Look closer. Look inside Bear and find Frog, and many others. This is where the story begins...

SUE COCCIA

Long ago, Bear lived on the edge of the world, where the land greeted the water and all the animals lived. Some animals lived in the sea, others in the air, and a few, like Bear, lived on the land and water.

One beautiful summer day, Bear came to her favorite place on the bank of the Great River. She loved this place because it was plentiful with huge shiny blackberries. Lifting her nose high in the air, she found her place by following the sweet smell of blackberries coming from the dense brambles. She wiggled through them to the edge of the river. From her favorite place, she watched everything unfold.

Grandmother Bear sat near Bear's favorite place. Bear loved her very much, and she scooted close to Grandmother and leaned on her while watching the world and listening to her stories. Bear soon became sleepy, so she closed her eyes and allowed a wondrous dream to unfold as Grandmother told a beautiful story about the many other animals that lived in the world.

SUE COCCIA

Of course, first was Salmon, an abundant fish. Grandmother told of Salmon's instincts and perseverance, and of how he and the others traveled many miles from the sea back to their home in the river where they were born. Bear dreamed of swimming upstream with many brothers and sisters. The water was cool, bubbly, and alive. The journey was long and full of twists and turns through the dancing waters. Big jumps were needed to swim upstream through the swift water flowing over the rocks. Bear thought of how Salmon never forgot his goal of reaching his home, and how hard the journey was. Bear gave thanks to Salmon and his comrades for their will to survive.

SUE COCCIA

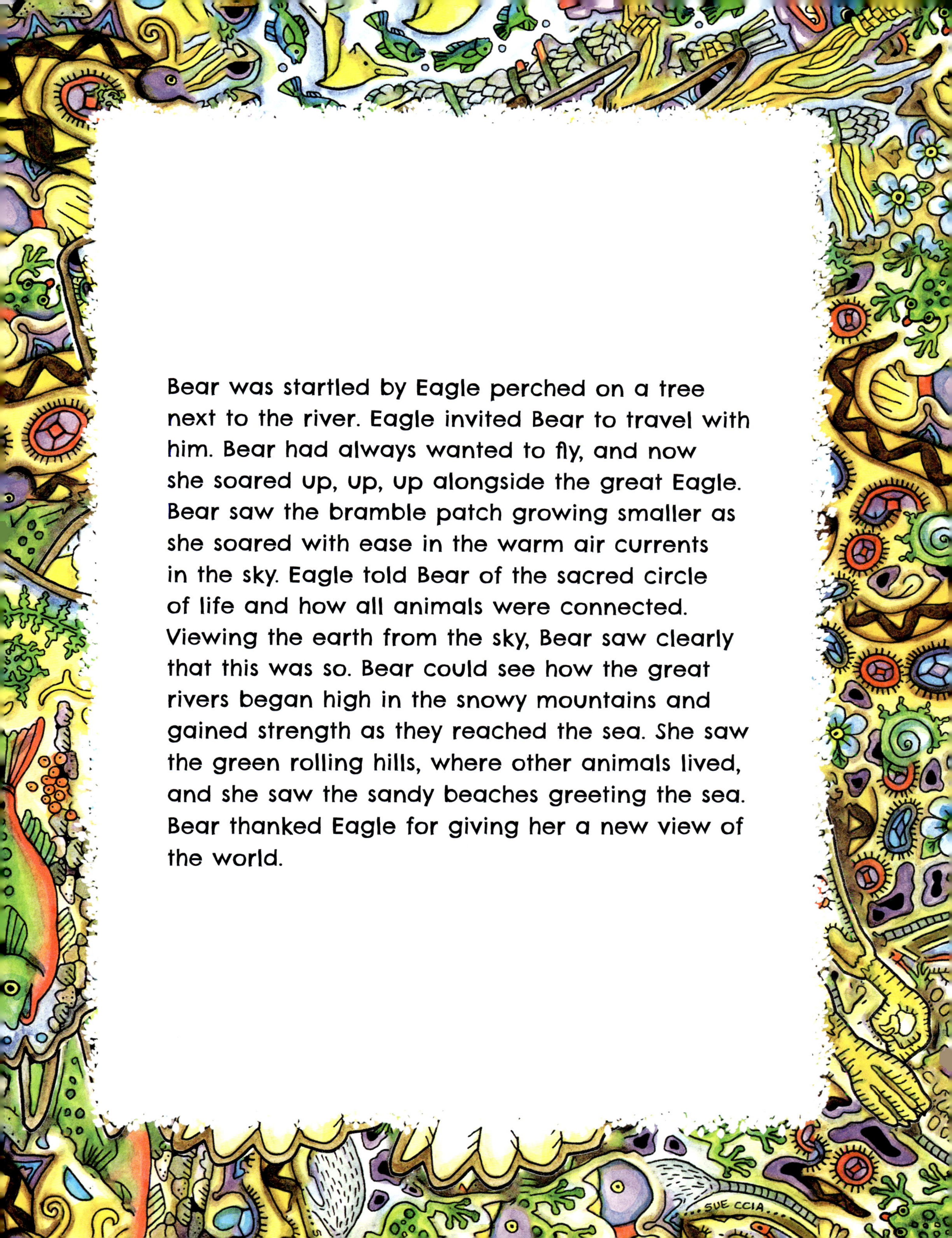

Bear was startled by Eagle perched on a tree next to the river. Eagle invited Bear to travel with him. Bear had always wanted to fly, and now she soared up, up, up alongside the great Eagle. Bear saw the bramble patch growing smaller as she soared with ease in the warm air currents in the sky. Eagle told Bear of the sacred circle of life and how all animals were connected. Viewing the earth from the sky, Bear saw clearly that this was so. Bear could see how the great rivers began high in the snowy mountains and gained strength as they reached the sea. She saw the green rolling hills, where other animals lived, and she saw the sandy beaches greeting the sea. Bear thanked Eagle for giving her a new view of the world.

SUE COCCIA

As Bear slowly glided to earth, Butterfly fluttered past. Oh, Butterfly was so beautiful! Grandmother had told Bear of Butterfly's great spirit, and Bear laughed. How could such a delicate creature be a great spirit? Butterfly explained how she started as a little caterpillar, enclosed by a cover called a cocoon, and she waited until she grew wings. Changing and growing was important. Bear was thankful for Butterfly's story and for the beauty she gave to the world.

Sue Coccia

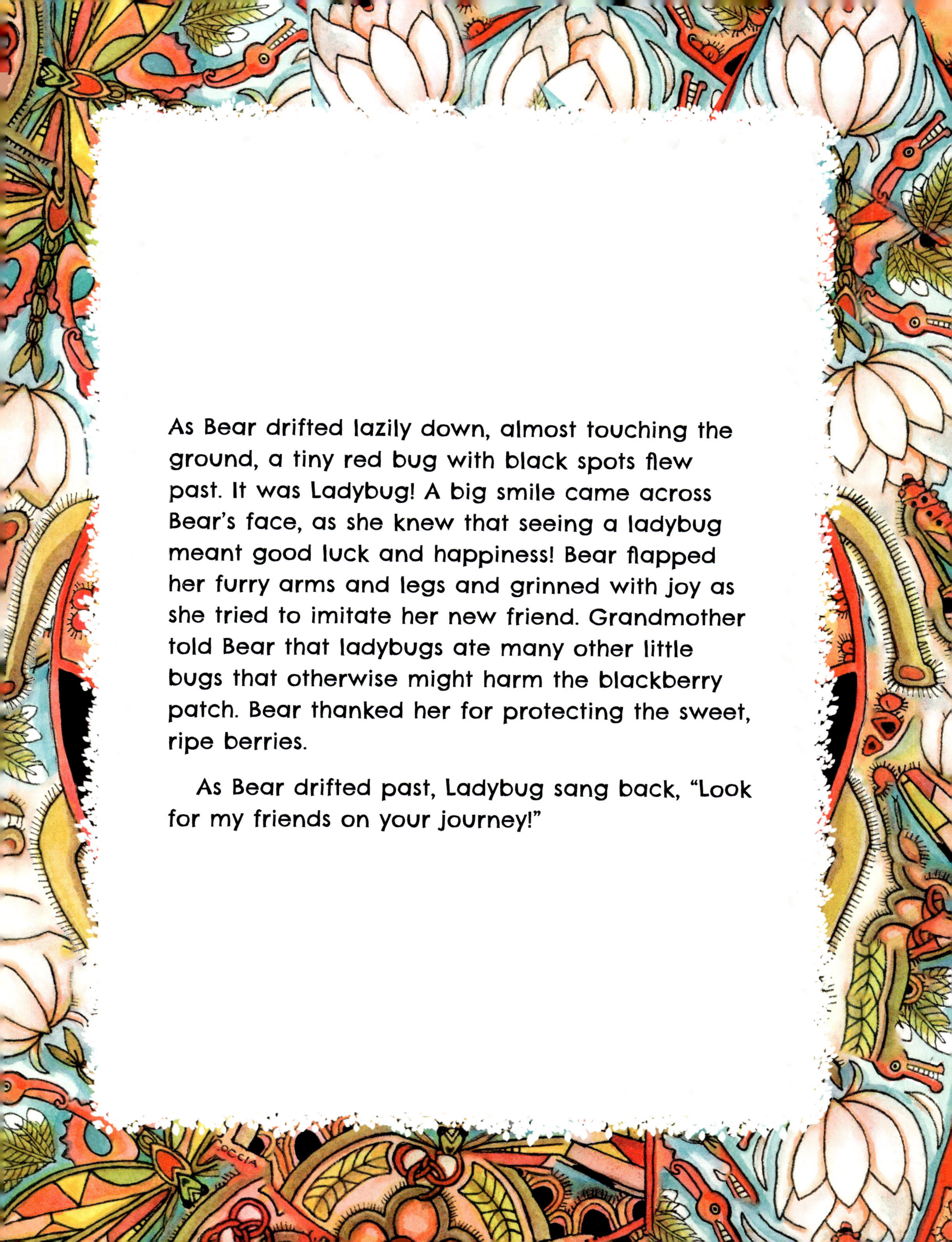

As Bear drifted lazily down, almost touching the ground, a tiny red bug with black spots flew past. It was Ladybug! A big smile came across Bear's face, as she knew that seeing a ladybug meant good luck and happiness! Bear flapped her furry arms and legs and grinned with joy as she tried to imitate her new friend. Grandmother told Bear that ladybugs ate many other little bugs that otherwise might harm the blackberry patch. Bear thanked her for protecting the sweet, ripe berries.

As Bear drifted past, Ladybug sang back, "Look for my friends on your journey!"

SUE COCCIA

"Caw, caw, caw," Bear heard. She looked up and saw Raven. Raven knew all of the languages and was a very good friend of the Bear Clan. Bear admired Raven's shiny black feathers and graceful flight. Raven asked Bear to join him while he flew to the coast. Raven told Bear it was important to never forget dreams and not to be afraid of the dark. As they approached the coast, Bear looked down and saw fountains of water coming up from the sea. "What is this?" she wondered. A huge black-and-white fish-like animal–an orca–leapt out of the sea and almost touched Bear. Bear was very frightened.

Raven said, "Don't be afraid of what you don't know. Goodbye now, Bear."

SUE COCCIA

As Raven flew away, Orca greeted Bear in a strange language. Bear was nervous because Orca was ten times larger than her and also had a big smiling mouth full of large white teeth! Bear floated down to the top of the sea and carefully approached Orca. Orca explained that he was not a fish but a mammal like Bear, and that he also belonged to a clan. Soon Bear felt less fear and joined her new friend Orca for a swim. Orca told Bear that whales and dolphins had special ways to talk to each other to find food and to help them travel great distances. Bear heard strange but lovely clicks and squeaks under the water. All at once, there came a booming *blllooottttweee,* and Bear swam quickly back up to the surface.

"Don't be afraid, little Bear," Orca said. He explained that his granny was coming to greet her. Granny was very old and very large. Bear felt a coziness wash over her, like when she fell asleep in her own grandmother's lap. Granny asked Bear if she would like to meet the shy octopus. Bear said yes and thanked her orca friends for making her feel at home with their family.

SUE COCCIA ©

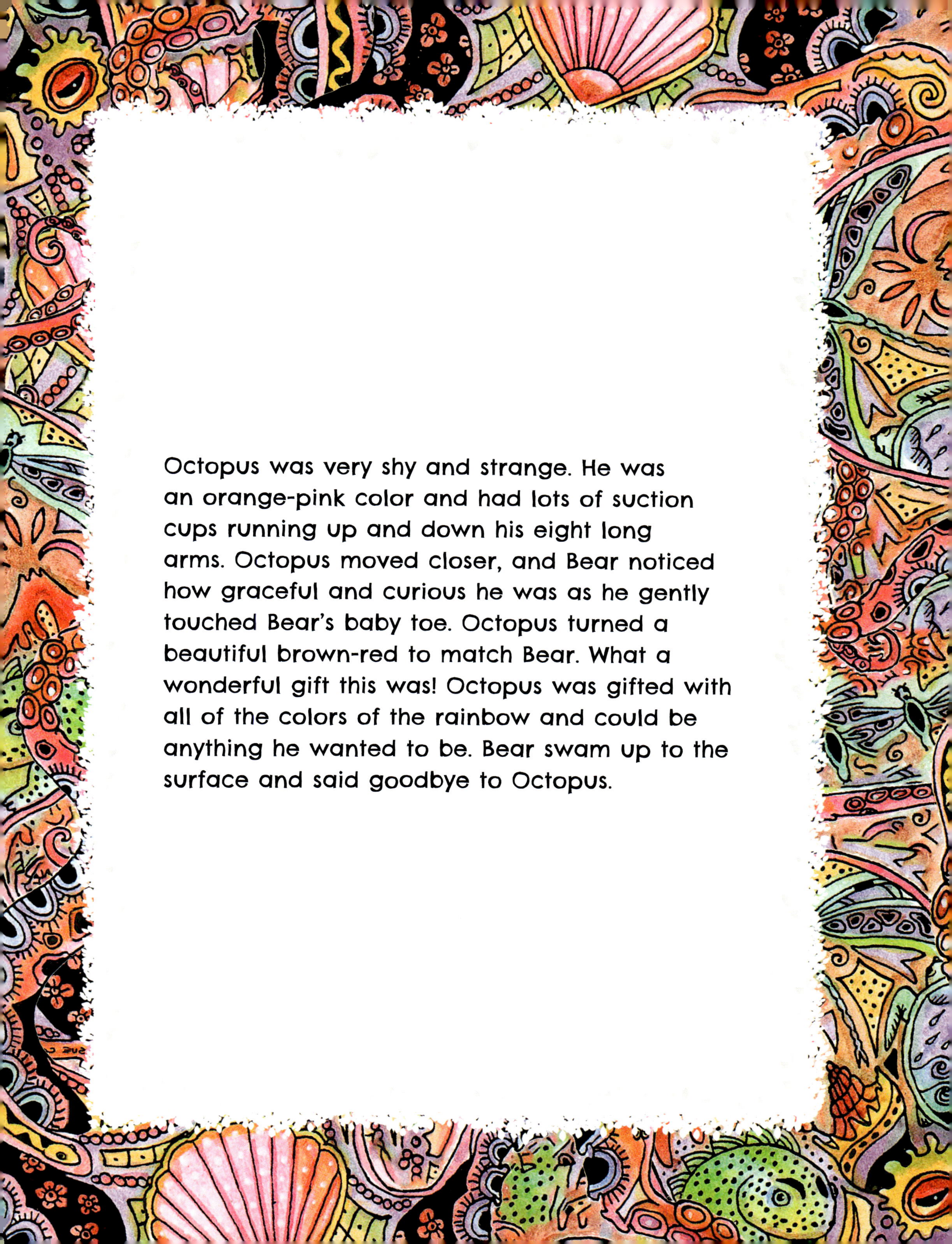

Octopus was very shy and strange. He was an orange-pink color and had lots of suction cups running up and down his eight long arms. Octopus moved closer, and Bear noticed how graceful and curious he was as he gently touched Bear's baby toe. Octopus turned a beautiful brown-red to match Bear. What a wonderful gift this was! Octopus was gifted with all of the colors of the rainbow and could be anything he wanted to be. Bear swam up to the surface and said goodbye to Octopus.

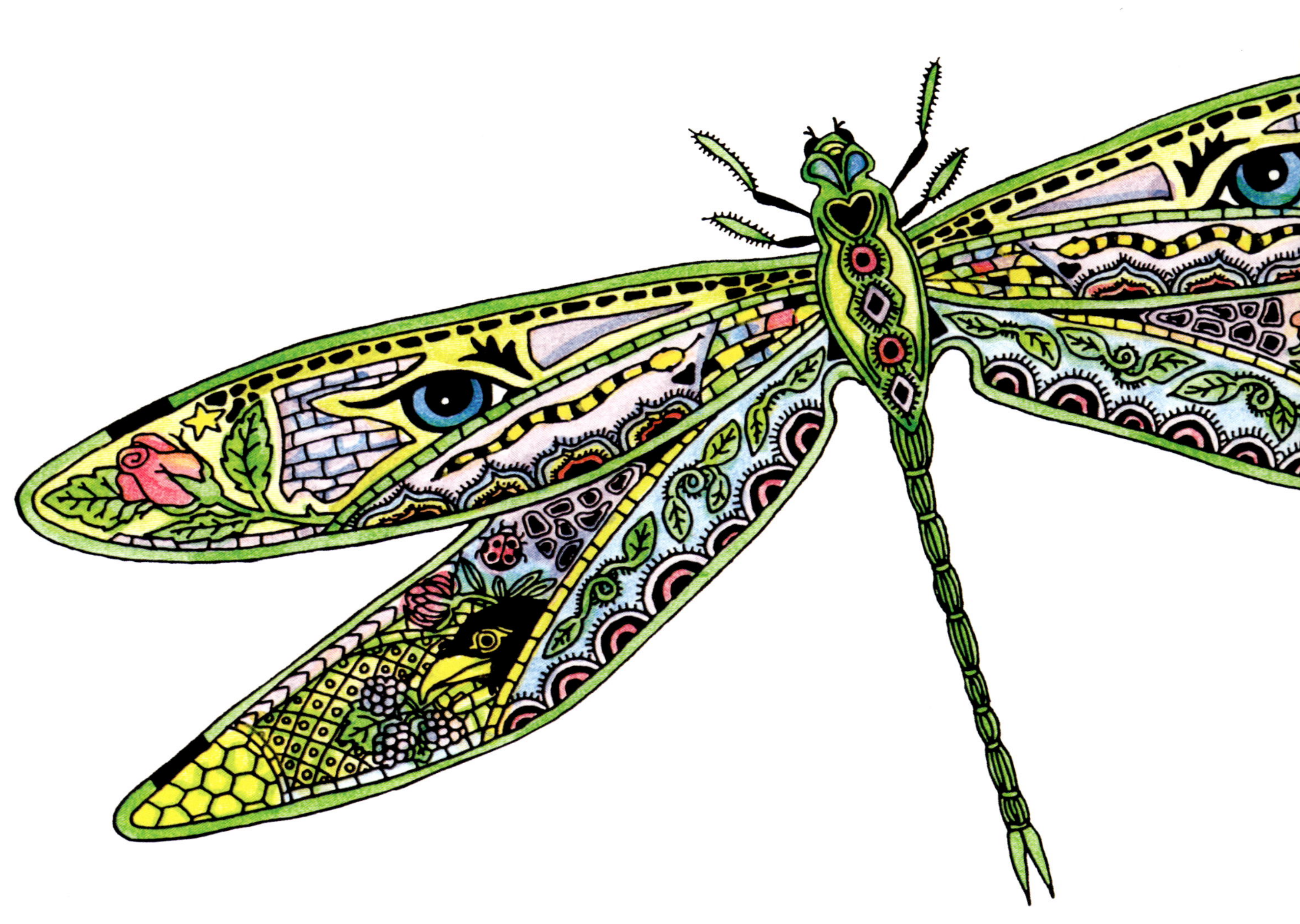

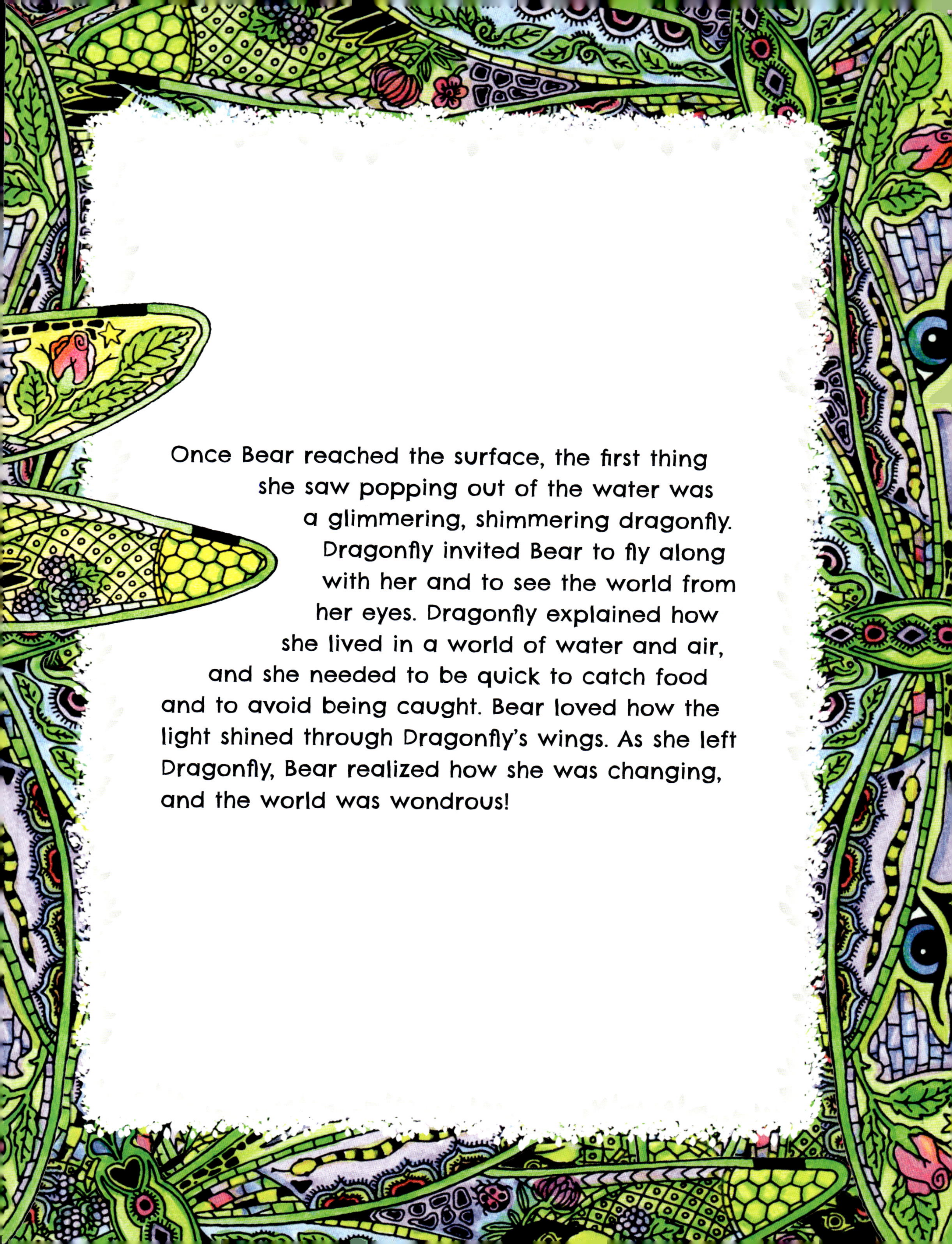

Once Bear reached the surface, the first thing she saw popping out of the water was a glimmering, shimmering dragonfly. Dragonfly invited Bear to fly along with her and to see the world from her eyes. Dragonfly explained how she lived in a world of water and air, and she needed to be quick to catch food and to avoid being caught. Bear loved how the light shined through Dragonfly's wings. As she left Dragonfly, Bear realized how she was changing, and the world was wondrous!

SUE COCCIA © 2001

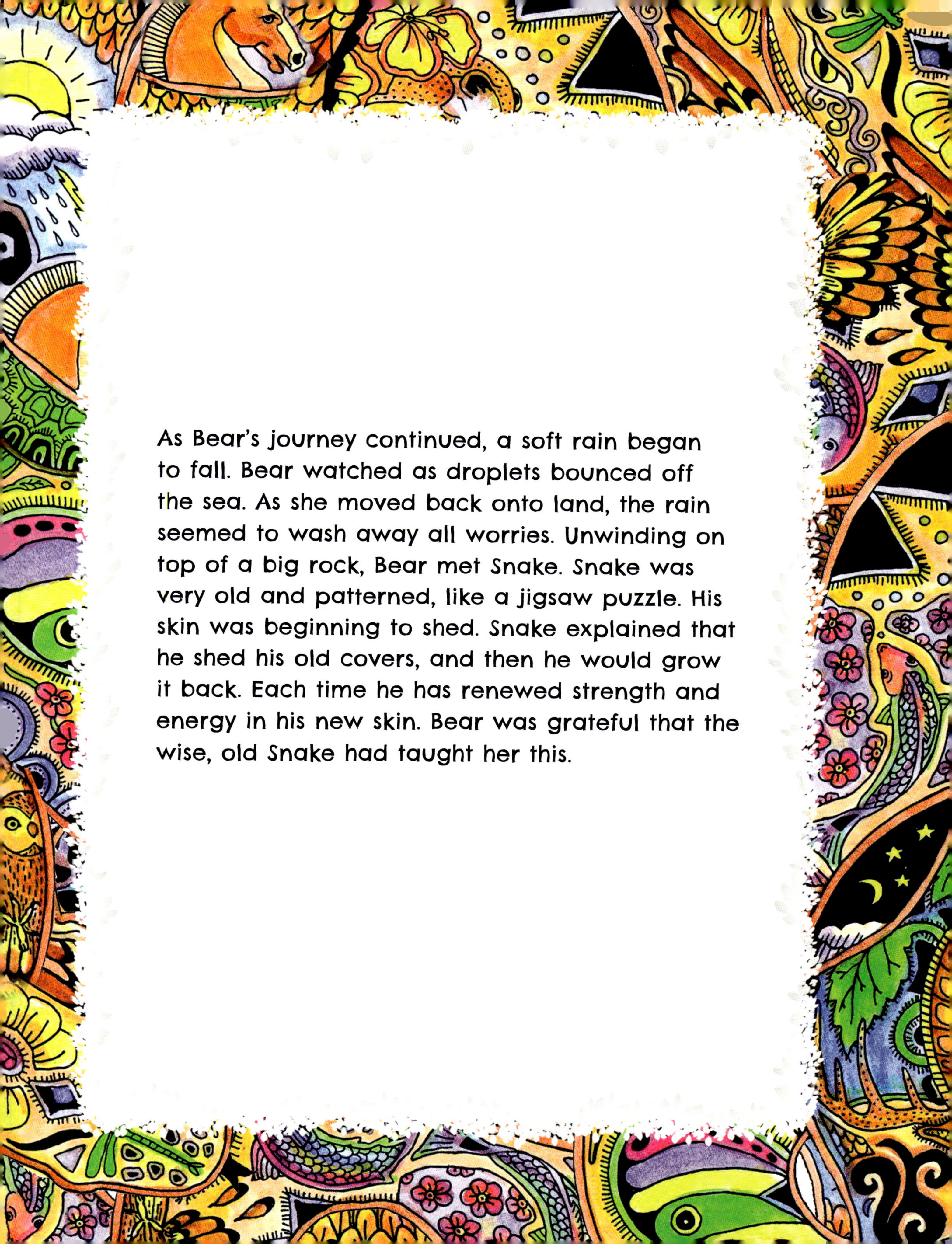

As Bear's journey continued, a soft rain began to fall. Bear watched as droplets bounced off the sea. As she moved back onto land, the rain seemed to wash away all worries. Unwinding on top of a big rock, Bear met Snake. Snake was very old and patterned, like a jigsaw puzzle. His skin was beginning to shed. Snake explained that he shed his old covers, and then he would grow it back. Each time he has renewed strength and energy in his new skin. Bear was grateful that the wise, old Snake had taught her this.

SUE COCCIA

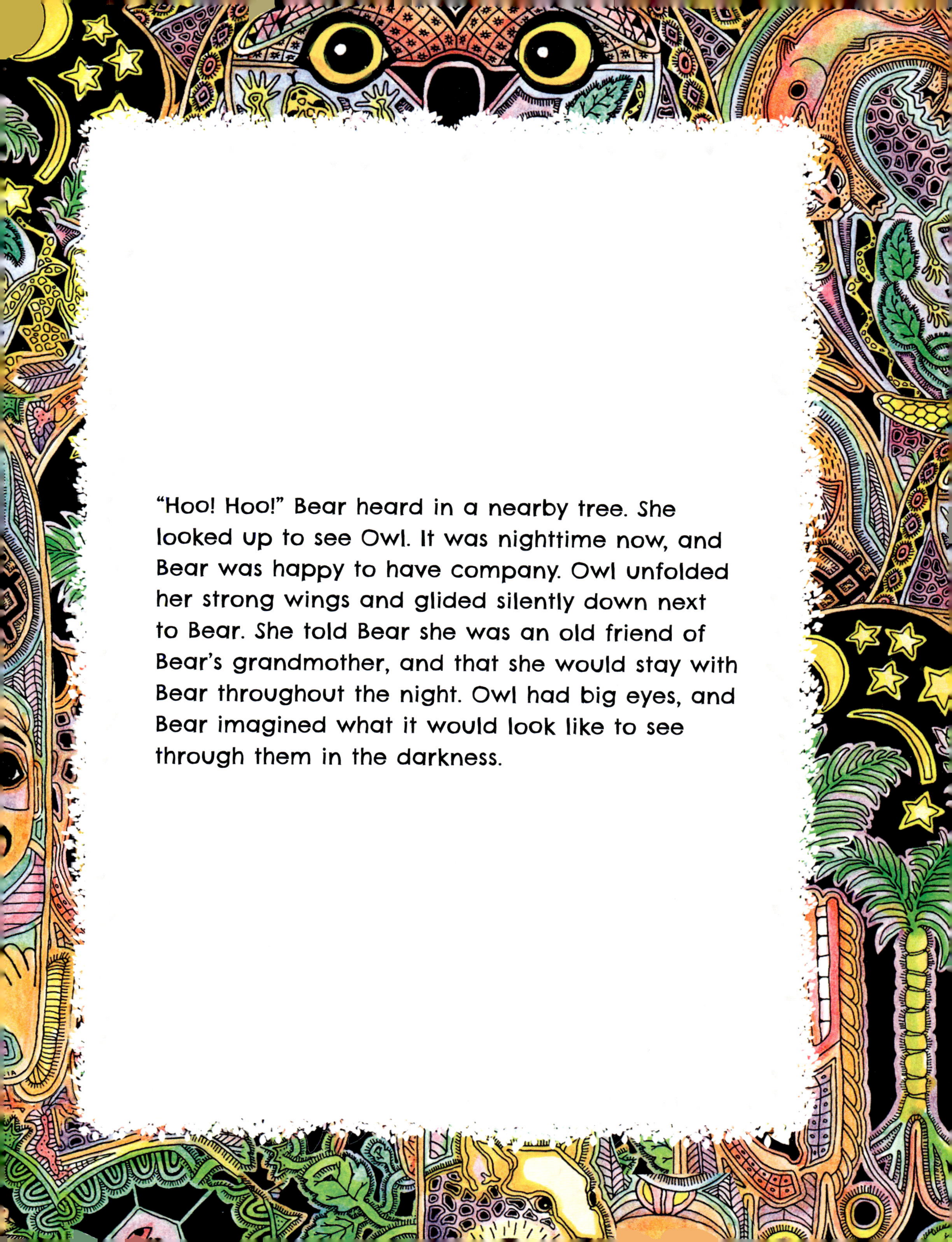

“Hoo! Hoo!” Bear heard in a nearby tree. She looked up to see Owl. It was nighttime now, and Bear was happy to have company. Owl unfolded her strong wings and glided silently down next to Bear. She told Bear she was an old friend of Bear’s grandmother, and that she would stay with Bear throughout the night. Owl had big eyes, and Bear imagined what it would look like to see through them in the darkness.

SUE COCCIA

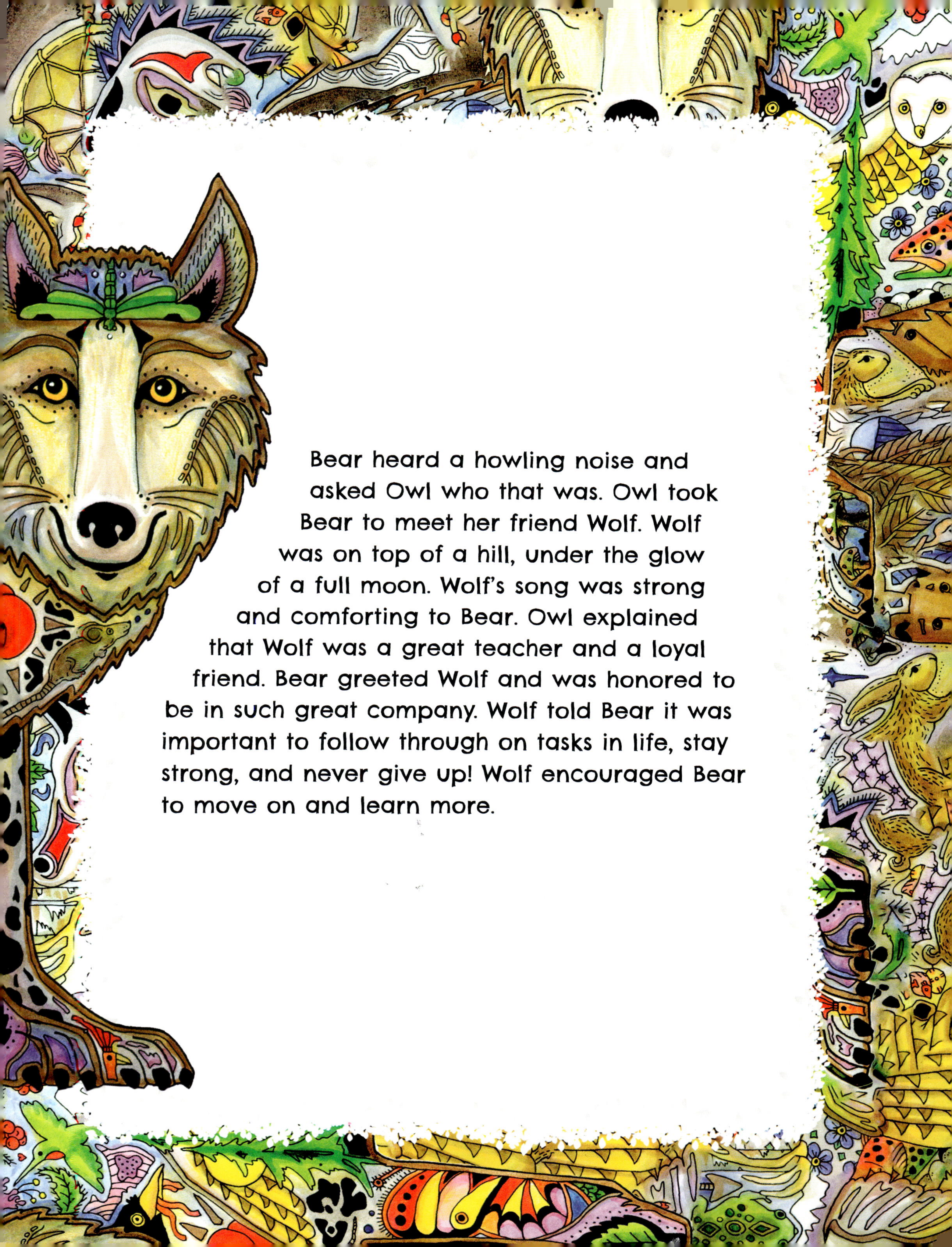

Bear heard a howling noise and asked Owl who that was. Owl took Bear to meet her friend Wolf. Wolf was on top of a hill, under the glow of a full moon. Wolf's song was strong and comforting to Bear. Owl explained that Wolf was a great teacher and a loyal friend. Bear greeted Wolf and was honored to be in such great company. Wolf told Bear it was important to follow through on tasks in life, stay strong, and never give up! Wolf encouraged Bear to move on and learn more.

SUE COCCIA ©

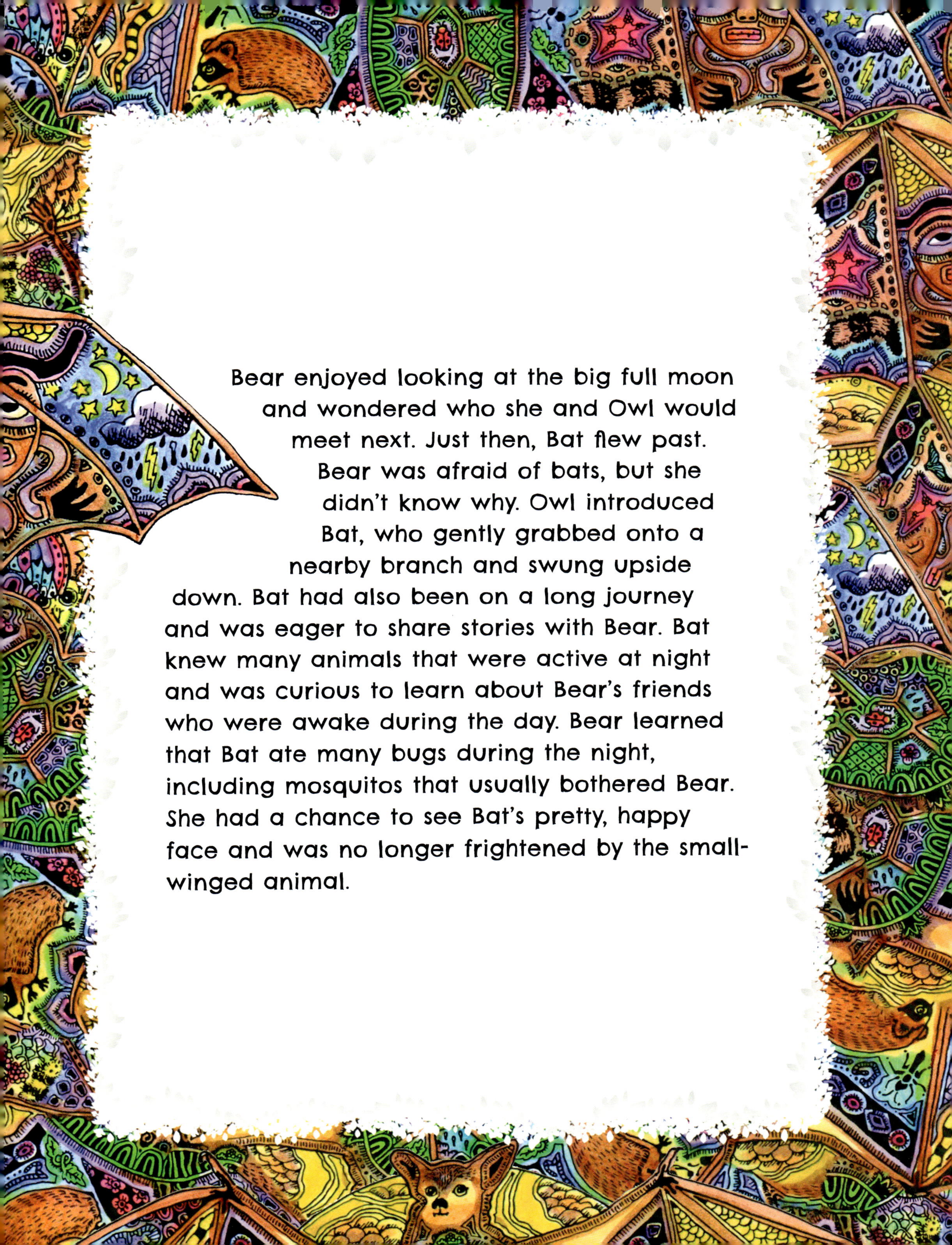

Bear enjoyed looking at the big full moon and wondered who she and Owl would meet next. Just then, Bat flew past. Bear was afraid of bats, but she didn't know why. Owl introduced Bat, who gently grabbed onto a nearby branch and swung upside down. Bat had also been on a long journey and was eager to share stories with Bear. Bat knew many animals that were active at night and was curious to learn about Bear's friends who were awake during the day. Bear learned that Bat ate many bugs during the night, including mosquitos that usually bothered Bear. She had a chance to see Bat's pretty, happy face and was no longer frightened by the small-winged animal.

SUE COCCIA©

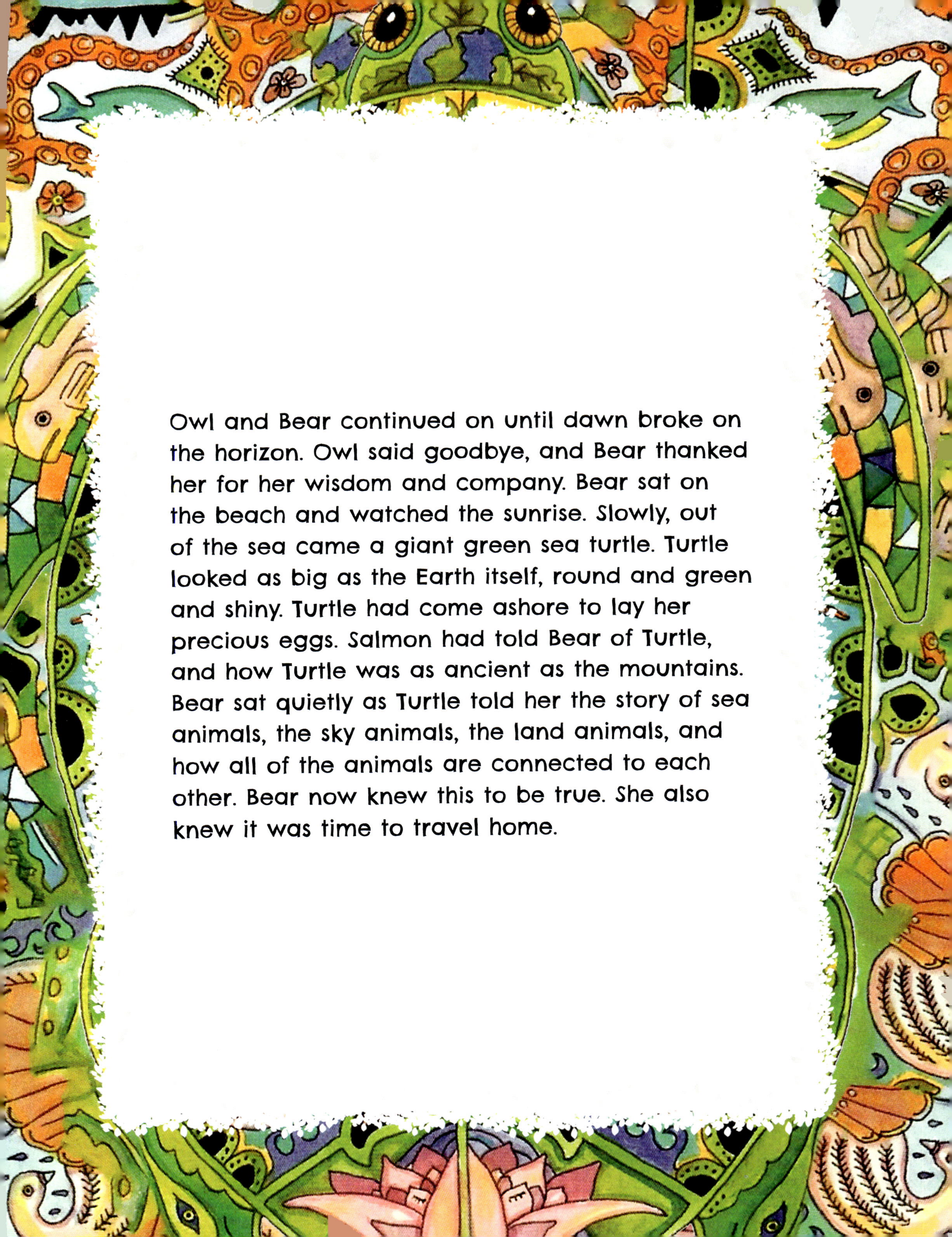

Owl and Bear continued on until dawn broke on the horizon. Owl said goodbye, and Bear thanked her for her wisdom and company. Bear sat on the beach and watched the sunrise. Slowly, out of the sea came a giant green sea turtle. Turtle looked as big as the Earth itself, round and green and shiny. Turtle had come ashore to lay her precious eggs. Salmon had told Bear of Turtle, and how Turtle was as ancient as the mountains. Bear sat quietly as Turtle told her the story of sea animals, the sky animals, the land animals, and how all of the animals are connected to each other. Bear now knew this to be true. She also knew it was time to travel home.

As Bear neared her home on the river, she heard a loud buzzing sound. It was Bee! Bee was a familiar friend, and he always guided Bear to the sweetest blackberry honey. Bees work very hard just to produce a single drop of honey. Bear knew bees worked together and were good neighbors in the river community.

SUE COCCIA©

As Bear reached home, she noticed a tiny frog on her shoulder. She wondered how long Frog had been there. Frog had little saucer-shaped fingers and toes that stuck tightly to Bear's fur.

He croaked, "I have traveled with you the whole journey. Grandmother Bear asked me to go with you so that you would return home safely."

Bear was glad to be home and found herself curled up snugly next to her grandmother. Bear thought of all the animals that she'd met on her journey. She was grateful to them for teaching her such wonderful and important lessons. She understood that each one of them had special gifts just like her! Bear smiled as she slowly closed her eyes, and Grandmother began another story.

EarthArt

Sue Coccia is the artist behind EarthArt International, a company that proudly supports the conservation of endangered species and their habitats, located in Edmonds, WA, where Sue is from. Animals are in desperate need of protection, mostly from loss of habitat. By raising awareness and encouraging people to understand that we are all connected, Sue is bringing people and nature together, for we all share the same space.

www.earthartinternational.com

Orca Network

Five percent of the profits from the sale of this book will be donated to the Orca Network in memory of Granny, J2.

The orca is the largest member of the dolphin family, and this particular orca, "Granny" (J2), was the oldest on record. As the leader of the endangered, southern resident killer whale population, Granny lived in the northeast Pacific Ocean and coastal bays of Washington State and British Columbia. Granny was estimated to have been born in 1911. She was last seen on October 12, 2016. Today, the southern residents are facing extinction due to a decline in their primary food source: Chinook salmon. Dam and fish farm removal must be taken seriously as soon as possible if they are to have any chance of recovering.

The orca culture is a matriarchal one, and, coincidentally, Granny had a half-moon notch in her dorsal fin (the crescent moon shape symbolizes the goddess). See within her environment the playful seal and the hiding frog. Also known as the sea wolf, she swims in pursuit of the Chinook salmon. Find the ladybug and she will bring you happiness and joy!

You can learn more about orcas by visiting www.orcanetwork.org.